Called to Serve

Becoming a Minister of the Gospel

Volume 1

Elder Joel Latimore Jr.

Called to Serve

Becoming a Minister of the Gospel

Volume 1

Written by Eld Joel Latimore Jr.

© 2026 Eld Joel Latimore Jr.

Latimore Publishing

ISBN (paperback): 979-8-218-89224-1

All rights reserved. No part of this book may be reproduced, stored in a retrieval system, or transmitted in any form or by any means—electronic, mechanical, photocopying, recording, or otherwise—without the prior written permission of the publisher, except for brief quotations used in reviews or scholarly works.

Scripture quotations are taken from the King James Version (KJV) of the Bible, unless otherwise noted.

EPIGRAPH

"For ye see your calling, brethren, how that not many wise men after the flesh, not many mighty, not many noble, are called:

But God hath chosen the foolish things of the world to confound the wise; and God hath chosen the weak things of the world to confound the things which are mighty."

— 1 Corinthians 1:26–27

TABLE OF CONTENTS

- Dedication

- Preface

Introduction   **Pg 1**

Ch 1 Understanding the call of God   **Pg 17**

Ch 2 The Minister's Character…   **Pg 45**

Ch 3 Consecration, Separation, …   **Pg 71**

Ch 4 The Minister's Private Life…   **Pg 98**

Ch 5 Faithfulness and Stewardship…	**Pg 122**
Ch 6 Guarding Doctrine, Truth…	**Pg 165**
Ch 7 Endurance, Patience …	**Pg 127**
Ch 8 Faithfulness Before Function	**Pg 190**
Ch 9 When the Call Confronts	**Pg 214**
Ch 10 The Minister Within the Body…	**Pg 239**
Ch 11 Tested, Proven, And Entrusted	**Pg 268**
Ch 12 Remain Faithful: The Final…	**Pg 295**

- Epilogue   **Pg 317**

- About the Author   **Pg 321**

DEDICATION

To every man and woman who has heard the whisper of God's calling

and feels its weight resting upon their soul.

To those who have chosen obedience over comfort,

humility over recognition,

and servanthood over self.

To the ministers who labor quietly, pray faithfully,

and stand in the gap when no one is watching.

To the next generation of Gospel carriers—

those who refuse to handle the Word of God lightly,

and who are committed to living in such a way

that the ministry is not blamed.

And above all,

to Jesus Christ—

the pattern, the example, the Master,

and the One who still calls men and women to follow Him.

For this calling is not a title to carry—

it is a life to be lived, a burden to be borne,

and a trust that must be kept before God.

PREFACE

The call to ministry is one of the greatest honors a man or woman can receive, yet it is also one of the most solemn responsibilities a human soul will ever carry.

Ministry is not a profession one chooses, a platform to stand upon, or a title to be admired. It is a divine summons—a sacred assignment entrusted to imperfect vessels who must daily depend upon the grace and guidance of the Holy Ghost.

Those who step into ministry must understand from the beginning that God will hold them accountable for the work they claim He has called them to perform. This calling requires seriousness of heart, clarity of mind, and a willingness to forsake all and follow Christ without reservation.

CALLING IS THE BEGINNING—NOT THE COMPLETION

Many feel the stirring of God and assume they are ready.

But calling does not mean readiness—it marks the beginning of a process.

Before God uses a vessel, He shapes it.

Before He entrusts responsibility, He develops character.

Before He releases a minister publicly, He deals with them privately.

This process cannot be rushed, avoided, or replaced.

Those who move ahead of God's preparation often damage both themselves and the people they are called to serve.

THE TRUE NATURE OF MINISTRY

The minister of the Gospel is not called to comfort, applause, or self-promotion, but to obedience, sacrifice, humility, and service.

Ministry begins with servanthood.

Before any man can preach with authority, he must kneel with sincerity.

Before he can lead God's people, he must first learn to follow God.

A minister's life must be free from pride, performance, manipulation, and the desire for human praise. Flesh must be crucified, motives purified, and character strengthened—lest the ministry be blamed because of the one who carries the message.

THE REQUIREMENTS OF THE VESSEL

Ministry does not require degrees, titles, or formal recognition—but it does require maturity.

A minister must possess:

- A stable mind
- A steady spirit
- Emotional balance
- Personal discipline

Without these, judgment becomes clouded and decisions can wound the very souls we are called to strengthen.

The Lord does not require a perfect vessel—but He does require a prepared one.

FINANCIAL INTEGRITY AND MOTIVE

Financial integrity is essential. A minister who is not stable in this area becomes vulnerable to misusing the calling.

The Gospel is not a business, and the pulpit is not a marketplace.

God's servants must never appear to minister for profit or personal gain. Our assignment is to serve people, not to extract from them.

THE ABSOLUTE NECESSITY OF THE HOLY GHOST

Above all, ministry requires total reliance on the Holy Ghost.

He alone:

- equips
- strengthens
- corrects
- protects
- empowers

Without His voice, our sermons are empty.

Without His guidance, our decisions are flawed.

Without His presence, our work has no eternal value.

THE URGENCY OF THE ASSIGNMENT

Jesus is soon to return, and the task before us is urgent.

We are not merely called to preach—we are called to prepare.

To prepare hearts.

To prepare lives.

To prepare people to stand before God.

We are stewards of the Gospel and must handle this calling with reverence, holiness, and the fear of the Lord.

PURPOSE OF THIS BOOK

This volume is not designed to promote ministry, but to prepare the minister.

It lays the foundation for understanding:

- what the call truly is

- what it requires

- how God shapes those He chooses

This is not about position—it is about preparation.

FINAL CHARGE

If God has called you, take this seriously.

Do not rush what God is still shaping.

Do not assume readiness because you feel desire.

Do not attempt to represent Christ without first surrendering fully to Him.

Let God prepare you.

For to serve Him is the highest honor—

and the greatest responsibility—you will ever carry

— Elder Joel Latimore Jr.

INTRODUCTION

The decision to enter ministry must never be taken lightly.

When a man or woman says, *"The Lord has called me,"*

they are not making a casual statement—**they are accepting responsibility for souls, for truth, and for representing Christ before His people.**

Ministry is not an occupation.

It is a divine trust.

DESIRE IS NOT THE SAME AS CALLING

Many feel a desire to preach.

Others feel a burden to serve.

Some feel a strong inward pull toward ministry.

But feeling something is not the same as being called.

And being called is not the same as being ready.

This is where many go wrong.

Emotion is mistaken for calling.

Excitement is mistaken for anointing.

Opportunity is mistaken for appointment.

But true calling is confirmed over time—through testing, shaping, correction, and submission to God.

MINISTRY IS NOT WHAT MANY THINK

Ministry is not:

- a platform

- a position

- a title

- a means of recognition

Ministry is service.

It is responsibility.

It is accountability.

It is representing Christ in word, conduct, and character.

A true minister does not seek to be seen—

he seeks to be faithful.

THE PROCESS CANNOT BE SKIPPED

Before God uses a man, He prepares him.

Before He sends him, He shapes him.

Before He entrusts him with people, He deals with his heart.

This process is not optional.

It is often slow.

It is often uncomfortable.

It is often hidden.

But it is necessary.

Those who bypass this process often become unstable, ineffective, and harmful to others.

God is not in a hurry—

but He is always intentional.

JESUS' PATTERN FOR MINISTRY

Before Jesus released His disciples into public ministry, He trained them.

Matthew chapters 5 through **7** are not simply instruction for believers—

they are the foundation for those who would represent Him.

MATTHEW 5 — CHARACTER

God shapes the inner life before assigning outward responsibility.

A minister must be:

- humble
- pure
- merciful
- spiritually hungry
- willing to endure

MATTHEW 6 — PRIVATE LIFE

Public ministry is built on private discipline.

A minister must learn to:

- pray without performance

- give without recognition

- fast without attention

- trust God for provision

MATTHEW 7 — ACCOUNTABILITY

Not everyone who ministers belongs to Christ.

Jesus warns that some will preach, prophesy, and perform works—

and still not know Him.

This is one of the most sobering truths in Scripture.

THE FOUNDATION OF TRUE MINISTRY

Ministry is not built on:

- charisma

- personality

- gifting

It is built on:

- character
- obedience
- discipline
- submission

A minister does not represent himself—he represents Christ.

PURPOSE OF THIS BOOK

This book is not written to excite you about ministry.

It is written to prepare you for it.

It will:

- define the calling
- expose misconceptions
- reveal the process
- establish the requirements

It will not rush you forward—

it will cause you to examine yourself.

FINAL CHARGE

If God has called you, do not treat it lightly.

Do not rush into position.

Do not assume readiness.

Do not confuse desire with calling.

Let God prepare you.

Because to be called is not to be ready—

it is to be claimed.

And those whom God claims,

He shapes, tests, and prepares until they can carry what He has entrusted to them.

CHAPTER 1

UNDERSTANDING THE CALL OF GOD

"And no man taketh this honour unto himself, but he that is called of God, as was Aaron."

— **Hebrews 5:4**

The Nature of the Call of God

The call of God is one of the most sacred realities a person can experience.

It is not inspiration.

It is not ambition.

It is not an interest in religious work.

The call of God is the divine summons of God upon a life.

When God calls a man or woman, He does not merely invite them into ministry—

He lays claim to their life for His purpose.

The call of God is not an addition to your life—

it is a surrender of it.

The Scriptures make it clear that no one appoints themselves to this work.

"And no man taketh this honour unto himself..."

Ministry is not self-appointed.

It is God-ordained.

WHAT THE CALL DOES

Throughout Scripture, those whom God called were never the same.

Abraham was called away from the familiar.

Moses was called from obscurity into confrontation.

Isaiah was undone by the holiness of God.

Paul was interrupted, transformed, and redirected.

A true call will change the direction of your life.

Priorities begin to shift.

Desires begin to change.

The things of God become greater than personal ambition.

The call is not just about what you will do—

it is about who you will become.

THE CALL TO SERVE, NOT TO BE SERVED

One of the most important truths every minister must understand is this:

Calling is not about being served—it is about serving.

When God calls a person, He is not granting them status.

He is entrusting them with responsibility.

Ministry is not about position, recognition, or influence.

Ministry is about service.

Jesus made this clear:

"For even the Son of man came not to be ministered unto, but to minister..."
— **Mark 10:45**

Though He was Lord of all, He chose humility.

He washed the feet of His disciples—

taking the place of the lowest servant.

"If I then, your Lord and Master, have washed your feet..."
— **John 13:14**

Ministry begins with a towel—not a title.

Those who are called must never forget:

they are servants of God and servants of His people.

CALLING DOES NOT EQUAL READINESS

Many feel something and assume they are ready.

But **calling is not readiness.**

Calling is the beginning of a process.

Throughout Scripture, we see this pattern:

Moses was called—but spent years in the wilderness.

David was anointed—but not immediately enthroned.

Joseph dreamed—but endured hardship before fulfillment.

Paul was called—but prepared before full release.

Between calling and assignment, there is preparation.

God uses this time to shape the vessel.

The call reveals God's intention.

Preparation develops God's servant.

Without preparation, calling can produce pride.

With preparation, calling produces stability and humility.

HOW A TRUE CALL IS RECOGNIZED

A true calling is not proven by words—it is revealed through evidence over time.

Many claim to be called, but few understand what that truly means.

A genuine call from God is marked by:

- Consistency — it does not fade with time or difficulty

- Conviction — it produces accountability before God

- Correction — God begins dealing with character and motives

- Submission — there is a willingness to be taught and shaped

- Separation — old desires begin to lose their hold

- Burden for souls — not just a desire to speak, but a concern for people

A true call will not only draw you forward—

it will begin to change you.

If what you call *"calling"* does not lead to transformation,

it must be examined.

THE WEIGHT OF THE CALLING

To be called by God is both a privilege and a responsibility.

Those who are entrusted with ministry are responsible for:

- teaching truth
- guiding people
- representing Christ

Because of this, ministry must never be approached carelessly.

Scripture warns:

"My brethren, be not many masters, knowing that we shall receive the greater condemnation."

— James 3:1

The call should not produce pride—

it should produce reverence.

A minister answers not only for what he says—

but for how he lives.

When God entrusts a person with souls,

He will hold them accountable.

THE MINISTER MUST GUARD HIS MOTIVES

Not all who preach are pure in heart.

Paul acknowledged that some preach from envy and strife.

This is why every minister must examine themselves:

- Why am I doing this?

- Am I seeking recognition?

- Am I craving influence?

- Am I trying to be seen?

A person can preach truth—and still have wrong motives.

God does not only examine the message—

He examines the heart.

THE CALL AND THE HOLY GHOST

The call of God cannot be fulfilled in human strength.

It must be carried by the Holy Ghost.

Jesus said:

"Without Me ye can do nothing."

— John 15:5

The Holy Ghost is the One who:

- shapes the heart

- corrects the life

- strengthens the servant

- gives discernment

- empowers the ministry

Without the Holy Ghost, calling becomes effort without power.

A minister must learn to depend on Him daily—

or the calling will become heavy, confusing, and unfruitful.

THE CALL MUST BE GUARDED

Paul told Timothy:

"Stir up the gift of God..."

— **2 Timothy 1:6**

A calling can grow cold if neglected.

It must be guarded through:

- prayer
- obedience
- discipline
- humility

The call is not sustained by emotion—it is sustained by faithfulness.

REFLECTIVE SUMMARY

The call of God is not initiated by human desire, ambition, or personal interest—it originates with God Himself. Scripture makes it clear that no one appoints themselves to this work. Those who are called are chosen and set apart by God for His purpose.

This chapter has shown that the call of God reshapes the life of the one who receives it. It is not merely about what a person will do, but about who they must become. True calling leads to surrender, humility, and obedience, and it is confirmed over time through transformation.

We have also seen that calling does not equal readiness. God prepares those He calls through seasons of shaping, testing, and correction.

Without this preparation, the calling can produce instability, but with it, the calling produces maturity and faithfulness.

The example of Jesus reminds us that ministry is rooted in servanthood, not status. Those who are called must guard their motives, recognizing that God examines not only what is done, but why it is done.

Finally, the call of God requires total dependence upon the Holy Ghost. Without Him, ministry becomes empty and ineffective. With Him, the servant is guided, strengthened, and empowered to carry the responsibility entrusted to them.

Understanding these truths provides a solid foundation for anyone who desires to serve faithfully in the work of the Lord.

CLOSING CHARGE

If God has called you, treat it with reverence and fear.

Do not rush what God is still shaping.

Do not assume readiness because you feel desire.

Do not attempt to represent Christ without surrendering fully to Him.

Do not measure your calling by visibility—

measure it by faithfulness.

Stay close to the Holy Ghost.

Submit to God's timing.

Remain faithful in your present season.

Because to be called is not to be finished—

it is to be claimed.

And those whom God calls,

He will examine—

to see how they carried what He placed upon their life.

REFLECTIVE QUESTIONS

1. When did you first become aware that God was calling you, and what confirmed that calling over time?

2. In what ways has the call of God begun to change your desires, priorities, and direction?

3. Are there areas in your life where God is currently preparing, correcting, or shaping you?

4. Do you view ministry as a position to step into or a responsibility to carry? Why?

5. How can you grow in your daily dependence on the Holy Ghost as you pursue your calling?

PRAYER

Heavenly Father,

Thank You for calling me to serve. Help me to walk in humility, guard me from pride, and teach me to trust Your process.

Shape my character, strengthen my faith, and guide me by the Holy Ghost, that I may serve with wisdom and integrity.

Let my life honor You.

In Jesus' Name, Amen.

CHAPTER 2

THE MINISTER'S CHARACTER, MINDSET, AND MATURITY

A divine calling requires a life that can carry that calling. The Lord never releases a minister based on excitement, emotion, or giftedness alone. He prepares the vessel before entrusting the work. This preparation begins with the shaping of character, for character is the invisible strength behind every visible assignment.

Character is what carries the calling when gifting cannot.

Paul wrote that a minister must be *"sober, just, holy, temperate"* **(Titus 1:8).**

He was not describing perfection; he was describing stability. A minister must be *dependable—steady in attitude, consistent in behavior*, and *reliable in judgment.* People cannot follow someone who cannot govern their own spirit.

Jesus spent years forming His disciples before sending them. He corrected them, tested them, instructed them, and revealed their weaknesses. Ministry today still requires that same process. A minister must allow the Holy Ghost to shape the inner life so the outer work can stand.

CHARACTER: THE SUBSTANCE BEHIND THE CALLING

Character is who a minister truly is when no one is present to applaud or criticize. It is shaped in *private prayer, personal decisions, quiet obedience,* and *surrendered moments before God.* A minister's character must reflect:

- Honesty

- Humility

- Purity

- Discipline

- Gentleness

- Patience

- Self-control

- Teachability

These qualities are not optional—they are foundational. Without them, ministry becomes unstable and unsafe.

These qualities determine the strength of one's ministry far more than talent or eloquence ever could.

Paul instructed Timothy: *"Take heed unto thyself"* **(1 Timothy 4:16).** Before a minister watches over others, he must watch over himself. *Self-examination, repentance, correction,* and *personal accountability* are vital to long-term effectiveness.

TEACHABILITY: A MARK OF TRUE MATURITY

One of the most overlooked ministerial traits is teachability. A minister must be able to receive instruction, correction, and guidance without becoming offended or defensive. Correction is not an insult—it is an investment.

Proverbs says, *"Reprove a wise man, and he will love thee"* **(Proverbs 9:8).**

A teachable minister:

- listens more than he speaks

- learns even from younger or less experienced believers

- does not resist counsel

- does not justify error

- does not fear being wrong

- values growth over image

A minister who cannot be corrected cannot be trusted.

This quality protects the minister from pride and allows God to shape him continually.

GENTLENESS: THE SPIRIT OF CHRIST IN MINISTRY

The Lord's worker cannot be harsh, domineering, or easily irritated. Paul wrote, *"The servant of the Lord must not strive; but be gentle unto all men"* **(2 Timothy 2:24).** Gentleness is not weakness; it is controlled strength. God's people are not to be driven—they are to be led.

A gentle minister:

- corrects without crushing

- speaks truth without belittling

- handles wounds carefully

- deals with conflict calmly

- treats people as souls, not obstacles

Harshness reveals insecurity—gentleness reflects Christ.

Authority in ministry is never an excuse for harshness.

SELF-DENIAL: REMOVING THE MINISTER FROM THE CENTER

Jesus made this requirement unmistakably clear:

"If any man will come after Me, let him deny himself" **(Matthew 16:24).**

Ministry dies the moment self is elevated. Self-glory, self-promotion, self-importance, and self-will have no place in the work of God.

A mature minister understands:

- the work is not about him

- the church does not belong to him

- the people are not his possessions

- the pulpit is not his stage

- the message is not his invention

Where self remains at the center, Christ is pushed to the margins.

The minister is a vessel—nothing more, nothing less.

SUBMISSION: LEARNING UNDER GODLY LEADERSHIP

God often shapes a minister through godly leaders, not isolation. Moses had Jethro. Joshua had Moses. Elisha had Elijah. Timothy had Paul. The disciples had Jesus.

Before a man can lead, he must first learn to follow.

Serving under godly leadership teaches:

- accountability
- reverence
- patience
- humility
- wisdom
- understanding of people
- how to handle pressure
- how to receive correction
- how to walk in unity

Scripture says, *"Whose faith follow"* **(Hebrews 13:7).**

A minister grows by observing faithfulness in others.

Those who refuse to follow well will never lead well.

EMOTIONAL AND MENTAL MATURITY

A minister must be able to carry burdens without collapsing, handle conflict without reacting in the flesh, and counsel others without being overwhelmed. Ministry requires sobriety of mind and steadiness of spirit.

The emotionally mature minister:

- does not overreact
- remains calm in crisis
- controls emotions under pressure
- forgives quickly

- avoids unnecessary arguments

- listens with patience

- thinks before speaking

Immaturity in the minister will eventually wound the people.

None of these skills are natural. They are formed through the *Holy Ghost, disciplined prayer,* and *continual surrender.*

DEPENDENCE ON THE HOLY GHOST

A minister cannot operate effectively in natural strength. Talents may impress people, but only the Holy Ghost transforms lives. Paul said, *"Our sufficiency is of God"* **(2 Corinthians 3:5).**

The Spirit must govern:

- the minister's thoughts

- his responses

- his preaching

- his decisions

- his counsel

- his discernment

- his endurance

Without the Holy Ghost, ministry becomes effort without power.

Without Him, ministry becomes heavy, draining, frustrating, and fruitless.

MATURITY: GROWING INTO THE ASSIGNMENT

Spiritual maturity is visible. Paul told Timothy, *"Give thyself wholly to them; that thy profiting may appear to all"* **(1 Timothy 4:15).**

A mature minister:

- admits mistakes

- seeks reconciliation

- asks questions

- listens deeply

- remains teachable

- walks consistently

- avoids extremes

- treats people with dignity

- refuses to retaliate

- prioritizes holiness

Maturity is not measured by how long you have been called—but by how well you have been formed.

Maturity is what God uses to sustain the calling placed on a minister's life.

REFLECTIVE SUMMARY

This chapter emphasizes that a divine calling must be supported by a life that has been shaped by God. Character, not gifting, is what sustains ministry over time. The minister must be stable, disciplined, teachable, and governed by the Spirit of God.

We have seen that true maturity is developed through correction, submission, and personal accountability. Traits such as gentleness, humility, and emotional stability are not optional—they are essential for effective ministry.

The chapter also highlights the importance of self-denial and submission to godly leadership. A minister must learn to follow before leading and must remove self from the center of ministry.

Finally, dependence on the Holy Ghost is necessary for every aspect of ministry. Without Him, the work becomes empty and ineffective. With Him, the minister is strengthened, guided, and sustained.

CLOSING CHARGE

Allow God to shape your character before you seek to shape the lives of others. Do not underestimate the importance of humility, teachability, and emotional maturity in ministry.

The gifts God gives you may open doors, but only character will sustain you once those doors open. Refuse to excuse immaturity, defensiveness, or instability as personality traits—these are areas God intends to refine.

Submit willingly to godly leadership and learn from those who walk faithfully before you. Resist the urge to lead before you have learned to follow. Cultivate gentleness, patience, and a listening spirit, for these qualities reflect the heart of Christ more than eloquence ever could. Do not strive for recognition; strive for faithfulness.

Above all, rely on the Holy Ghost. Let Him govern your responses, guide your decisions, and steady your inner life. Ministry carried in the flesh will always fail, but ministry carried in the Spirit will endure. Let God finish His work in you before He releases His work through you.

God is not preparing you for visibility—He is preparing you for responsibility.

REFLECTIVE QUESTIONS

1. In what areas is God currently developing your character, and how are you responding to that process?

2. Are you open to correction and instruction, or do you find yourself resisting it?

3. How do you handle emotional pressure, conflict, and responsibility in your current season?

4. In what ways can you grow in humility, gentleness, and self-denial?

5. How can you deepen your daily dependence on the Holy Ghost in your life and ministry?

PRAYER

Heavenly Father,

Thank You for shaping my life for Your purpose. Help me to grow in character, humility, and obedience.

Teach me to remain teachable, to walk in maturity, and to depend fully on the Holy Ghost.

Let my life reflect Your truth and honor You in all that I do.

In Jesus' Name, Amen.

CHAPTER 3

CONSECRATION, SEPARATION, AND THE COST OF FOLLOWING CHRIST

Every genuine call to ministry carries with it a call to consecration. God does not merely call His servants to do His work; He calls them to belong to Him.

Consecration is the act of being set apart for God's use—*holy, devoted,* and *yielded.* It is not a momentary decision but a lifelong posture of surrender.

Consecration is not optional for the minister—it is essential.

Consecration is not what you do occasionally—it is how you live continually.

From the earliest pages of Scripture, God's pattern is consistent: He separates before He sends. **Abram** was called out… **Moses** was separated… **Elijah** was hidden… **John the Baptist** lived apart… **Jesus** withdrew…

Separation, therefore, is not rejection; it is preparation.

The apostle Paul wrote plainly, *"Come out from among them, and be ye separate…"* **(2 Corinthians 6:17).**

This separation is not primarily geographical; it is spiritual and moral.

A minister cannot effectively confront darkness while embracing the same appetites and influences that produce it.

A servant cannot confront what he is unwilling to separate from.

THE NATURE OF SEPARATION

Separation does not mean isolation from people—it means distinction in character, values, and conduct.

God does not call His people to withdraw from society entirely, but He does call them to live differently within it.

Separation is not about losing identity—it is about discovering it in God.

The minister must be:

- set apart in thinking
- set apart in behavior
- set apart in desires
- set apart in priorities

This distinction becomes visible over time. It is not forced—it is formed.

HOLINESS: GOD'S STANDARD

Holiness is not a suggestion—it is a requirement.

God said, "Be ye holy; for I am holy" (1 Peter 1:16).

Holiness is not a preference—it is God's standard.

Holiness affects:

- speech
- conduct
- relationships
- decisions
- private life
- public life

It is not limited to appearance—it is a condition of the heart.

True holiness is not maintained by appearance—it is sustained by the condition of the heart.

A person can appear separated outwardly and still be compromised inwardly.

Compromise does not happen suddenly—it begins where separation is ignored.

Compromise rarely announces itself—it develops quietly over time.

A minister who neglects holiness weakens both his life and his ministry.

THE COST OF FOLLOWING CHRIST

Jesus made it clear that following Him comes with a cost:

"If any man will come after Me, let him deny himself..." **(Matthew 16:24)**

To follow Christ is to surrender personal rights, desires, and ambitions.

It may cost:

- relationships
- opportunities
- comfort
- reputation
- personal preferences

The call of God will cost you something—but it will never cost more than it is worth.

What you surrender for Christ is never wasted—it is transformed.

This cost is not punishment—it is purification.

WHEN SEPARATION INCLUDES PEOPLE

There are times when separation involves distancing from certain relationships.

Not all relationships can continue in the same way when a person is called to a higher level of consecration.

Not everyone can go where God is taking you.

This is not about rejecting people—it is about protecting purpose.

A minister must discern:

- which relationships strengthen
- which relationships distract
- which relationships hinder

Wisdom is required in handling these decisions with grace and humility.

SEPARATION IS NOT ISOLATION

While God calls His servants to be separate, He does not call them to be alone.

Isolation leads to imbalance, discouragement, and vulnerability.

God separates you from the world—but connects you to His people.

A minister still needs:

- fellowship
- accountability
- encouragement
- spiritual covering

Healthy relationships strengthen the servant and help maintain balance.

THE ROLE OF THE HOLY GHOST IN CONSECRATION

Consecration cannot be maintained in human strength.

The Holy Ghost works within the believer to:

- convict
- correct
- strengthen
- guide
- refine

The Holy Ghost forms the life of consecration by dealing with pride, correcting motives, and teaching obedience.

Without Him, separation becomes external and forced.

With Him, it becomes internal and genuine.

THE EVIDENCE OF A CONSECRATED LIFE

A consecrated life is not merely declared—it is demonstrated.

It is marked by:

- sensitivity to sin

- quick repentance

- guarded decisions

- hunger for God

- willingness to obey

Consecration reveals itself over time through consistent obedience and a heart that responds quickly to God.

FAITHFULNESS IN THE PROCESS

Consecration and separation are not one-time decisions—they are ongoing commitments.

The minister must remain faithful daily:

- in private devotion

- in personal conduct

- in obedience to God

- in resisting compromise

Consecration is sustained through daily discipline, not occasional decisions.

Growth in consecration happens over time.

It is not instant—it is developed.

What you allow in private will eventually appear in public.

REFLECTIVE SUMMARY

This chapter teaches that consecration and separation are essential aspects of the minister's life. God calls His servants not only to serve Him, but to belong to Him fully.

Consecration is not occasional—it is continual. It is a life set apart in heart, conduct, and conviction.

Separation is not about isolation—it is about distinction. Holiness is not optional, and compromise often begins quietly where separation is ignored.

We have also seen that following Christ comes with a cost. The call may require letting go of relationships, comforts, and personal desires, but what is surrendered is never wasted—it is transformed by God.

Finally, the Holy Ghost plays a vital role in sustaining consecration. He works within the believer to shape, correct, and guide the life of the minister.

CLOSING CHARGE

Remain faithful to the process of consecration.

Do not compromise in areas where God has called you to be set apart. Do not return to what God has delivered you from, and do not lower your standard to match those around you.

Walk in holiness, guard your heart, and remain committed to the life God has called you to live. Let your separation be evident not in appearance alone, but in character, conduct, and conviction.

What you refuse to let go of will eventually limit what God can do through you.

God does not entrust His work to those who want to be seen—but to those who are willing to be set apart.

God will not bless what you refuse to surrender.

REFLECTIVE QUESTIONS

1. In what areas is God calling you to deeper consecration?

2. Are there private areas of your life that need to be brought into alignment with God's standard?

3. Have you allowed small compromises that could grow over time?

4. What is God asking you to surrender in this season?

5. How can you strengthen your daily discipline and dependence on the Holy Ghost?

PRAYER

Heavenly Father,

Set my life apart for Your purpose. Help me to walk in holiness, guard my heart, and remain faithful to Your calling.

Give me strength to surrender what You require and discipline to live a life that honors You.

In Jesus' Name, Amen.

CHAPTER 4

THE MINISTER'S PRIVATE LIFE: PRAYER, DISCIPLINE, AND OBEDIENCE

Before God trusts a man in public, He tests him in private.

What a minister does when no one is watching will determine what he can carry when everyone is.

Public ministry is sustained—or sabotaged—by a minister's private life. **What is celebrated in public is formed in secret, and what collapses publicly usually eroded privately first.** Scripture consistently teaches that God works deepest in the unseen places, shaping His servants through prayer, discipline, and obedience long before He entrusts them with influence.

Scripture consistently reveals this pattern:

"But thou, when thou prayest, enter into thy closet..." **(Matthew 6:6)**

"Study to shew thyself approved unto God..." **(2 Timothy 2:15)**

"To obey is better than sacrifice..." **(1 Samuel 15:22)**

Jesus Himself modeled this pattern. Though crowds pressed Him daily, He repeatedly withdrew to solitary places to pray. **His power in public was rooted in His communion in private.** His authority was not manufactured—it was cultivated through consistent submission to the Father.

A minister who neglects the private life may still function outwardly for a season, but eventually, **what is hidden will be revealed.** God does not anoint what is unsubmitted, and **He does not sustain what is not rooted in Him.**

God develops His ministers in secret before He displays them in public.

PRAYER: THE FOUNDATION OF ALL TRUE MINISTRY

Prayer is not optional for the minister—it is essential.

It is through prayer that the servant of God receives direction, correction, strength, and clarity. **Without prayer, ministry becomes mechanical. With prayer, ministry remains spiritual.**

A minister who prays is not merely preparing sermons—**he is preparing his heart.**

In prayer, God:

- Exposes hidden motives

- Aligns the heart with His will

- Strengthens the inner man

- Gives wisdom beyond natural understanding

Prayer is where the minister is reminded that he is not the source—God is.

Without prayer, a minister may rely on experience, personality, or knowledge. But these cannot replace the guidance of the Spirit.

A minister who neglects prayer may still produce messages, but he will lack unction. Words may be spoken—but they will not carry weight.

A prayerless ministry may appear effective outwardly, **but it lacks the sustaining power of God.**

DISCIPLINE: THE STRUCTURE THAT SUSTAINS THE CALL

Discipline is what protects the calling.

Many desire the platform, but few embrace the discipline required to remain faithful. Spiritual discipline is not legalism—it is alignment. It positions the minister to remain sensitive to the Spirit and faithful to the assignment.

Discipline includes:

- Consistent time in the Word
- Guarding one's thoughts and actions
- Maintaining integrity in private conduct
- Resisting distractions and temptations

Discipline is often developed in the areas no one else sees—how a minister manages time, what he entertains in his mind, and what he allows to influence his spirit.

A lack of discipline leads to instability.

A disciplined life, however, produces consistency, and consistency builds trust—both with God and with those being led.

Ministry without discipline becomes unpredictable. But when discipline is present, there is order, stability, and endurance.

OBEDIENCE: THE TRUE EVIDENCE OF DEVOTION

Obedience is the clearest evidence of a surrendered life.

It is possible to pray and still resist God. It is possible to know Scripture and still walk in disobedience. But true ministry is marked by a willingness to obey—even when it is uncomfortable, unseen, or misunderstood.

God does not measure devotion by words alone, but by response.

Obedience often requires:

- Letting go of personal desires

- Accepting correction

- Following God's instruction without full understanding

- Remaining faithful in difficult seasons

The minister must learn that delayed obedience is still disobedience.

What God asks for is not partial surrender— but complete submission.

THE MINISTRY OF HIDDENNESS

Before God reveals a man, He often hides him.

There are seasons where God intentionally removes visibility, not as punishment, but as preparation.

In hiddenness:

- Character is refined
- Motives are purified
- Dependence on God is strengthened

Many desire to be seen, but few are willing to be developed in secret.

Hidden seasons are where God does His deepest work.

If a minister cannot be faithful when unseen, he will not be stable when exposed.

THE DANGER OF A NEGLECTED PRIVATE LIFE

When the private life is neglected, several dangers arise:

- **Spiritual dryness** — The minister continues outward activity but loses inward vitality

- **Compromise** — Small areas of disobedience begin to grow

- **Pride** — Success replaces dependence on God

- **Burnout** — Strength is drawn from self rather than from the Spirit

These dangers do not appear suddenly—they develop gradually.

What is ignored in private will eventually be exposed in public.

That is why the private life must be guarded intentionally.

No amount of public success can compensate for private failure.

DEVELOPING A STRONG PRIVATE LIFE

A strong private life does not happen by accident—it is developed through intentional commitment.

The minister must establish:

- A consistent prayer life

- A disciplined approach to Scripture

- A willingness to obey God daily

- A habit of self-examination before the Lord

Growth in private produces strength in public.

What God builds in secret, He can trust in the open.

WHEN NO ONE IS WATCHING

The true measure of a minister is not how he performs before others—but how he lives before God when no one is watching.

It is in the unseen moments that character is formed.

It is in the quiet places that convictions are strengthened.

It is in private obedience that public authority is established.

A minister must learn to value God's approval above all else.

Because in the end, it is not the applause of people that matters—it is the approval of God.

REFLECTIVE SUMMARY

The strength of a minister's public life is rooted in the condition of his private life. Prayer keeps the minister connected to God, discipline keeps him steady, and obedience keeps him aligned with God's will.

When these are neglected, ministry becomes unstable and vulnerable to compromise. But when they are cultivated, they produce endurance, clarity, and spiritual authority.

God develops His servants in secret so that they can stand in public without falling.

CLOSING CHARGE

Guard your private life with the same seriousness that you guard your public calling.

Do not allow activity to replace intimacy.

Do not allow visibility to replace integrity.

Commit yourself daily to prayer, discipline, and obedience.

Because what you become in private will determine what you can sustain in public.

Do not build a ministry that your private life cannot sustain.

REFLECTIVE QUESTIONS

1. Is my prayer life consistent, or only active when I am under pressure?

2. Are there areas of my life where discipline is lacking?

3. Am I obeying God fully, or only in the areas that are comfortable?

4. What habits am I building in private that will affect my public ministry?

5. Do I value God's approval more than the recognition of others?

PRAYER

Lord, help me to guard my private life before You. Teach me to pray with sincerity, to live with discipline, and to walk in full obedience to Your will.

Search my heart and reveal anything that is not aligned with You.

Strengthen me in the hidden places, so that my life may reflect Your truth both in private and in public.

In Jesus' Name, Amen.

CHAPTER 5

FAITHFULNESS AND STEWARDSHIP: GUARDING THE TRUST OF THE CALLING

God does not reward faithfulness—He requires it.

Before God entrusts a minister with people, influence, or responsibility, He entrusts that minister with faithfulness.

Faithfulness is not measured by visibility, position, or results—it is revealed through consistency, obedience, and how you handle what no one else sees. In the early stages of calling, faithfulness is primarily inward before it is outward.

Scripture declares, *"Moreover it is required in stewards, that a man be found faithful"* **(1 Corinthians 4:2).**

A steward manages what belongs to another. At this stage, the minister is not managing people or platforms, but the calling itself—**guarding it, honoring it, and preparing to carry it without corruption.**

God trusts faithful men with weighty assignments.

UNDERSTANDING STEWARDSHIP AT THE BEGINNING OF THE CALL

In **Volume 1,** stewardship must be understood as personal responsibility, not public authority. God examines how a person handles:

- their time

- their obedience

- their discipline

- their integrity

- their motives

- their private decisions

- their reverence for holy things

Before God enlarges responsibility, He watches how His servant handles small, unseen trusts.

The parable of the talents teaches that God expects growth and responsibility, even when the assignment appears small (Matthew 25:14–30). Neglect, fear, or carelessness at this stage delays preparation.

A faithful minister understands that the calling is not owned—it is carried.

FAITHFUL IN THE UNSEEN AND THE ORDINARY

Jesus said, *"He that is faithful in that which is least is faithful also in much"* **(Luke 16:10).**

Early faithfulness often looks ordinary: prayer when no one is watching, obedience without recognition, discipline without applause, and restraint when compromise would be easy.

At this stage, faithfulness shows itself in:

- consistency in prayer
- seriousness about Scripture
- reliability in commitments

- honesty in speech

- purity in conduct

- patience in waiting

- obedience in small instructions

God often withholds greater responsibility not as punishment, but as protection—until faithfulness becomes settled character.

THE DANGER OF UNFAITHFULNESS

Unfaithfulness rarely begins publicly—it begins privately.

It shows up in:

- neglected prayer

- careless obedience

- ignored conviction

- compromised integrity

What is mishandled in private will eventually be exposed in public.

A minister who is careless with small responsibilities cannot be trusted with greater ones.

STEWARDSHIP OF MOTIVES AND DESIRES

One of the earliest tests of faithfulness is motive. A minister must examine why they desire ministry and what they expect from it. Paul warned against those who serve *"supposing that gain is godliness"* **(1 Timothy 6:5).**

Even sincere servants must guard against ambition, comparison, and the craving for recognition.

God will often delay visibility to expose motive.

At this stage, stewardship includes:

- surrendering the desire to be seen
- releasing timelines and expectations
- resisting comparison with others
- trusting God's pace
- embracing hidden seasons

God is more concerned with who you are becoming than when you will be seen.

STEWARDSHIP OF PERSONAL INTEGRITY

Integrity is the alignment between belief and behavior. A minister's private choices matter deeply, even before public ministry begins.

Scripture warns, *"Take heed unto thyself"* **(1 Timothy 4:16).** This instruction comes before teaching others.

Integrity is who you are when there is no consequence for doing wrong.

Faithfulness requires guarding:

- moral boundaries
- speech and attitudes
- thought life
- emotional responses
- personal conduct

Compromise at the beginning weakens discernment later. Integrity formed early becomes protection in future seasons.

FAITHFULNESS AS PREPARATION, NOT PROMOTION

In **Volume 1,** faithfulness is not a pathway to promotion—it is a pathway to preparation.

God uses faithfulness to stabilize the heart, mature the mind, and strengthen the spirit.

Those who rush ahead often bypass the very formation that would sustain them later.

Paul's testimony—*"I have kept the faith"* **(2 Timothy 4:7)**—was not about accomplishment, but endurance.

Faithfulness means remaining obedient even when progress feels slow and direction feels unclear.

GOD WATCHES HOW THE CALL IS CARRIED

The Lord watches how His servants treat the calling while it is still forming.

Faithfulness at this stage communicates reverence. Carelessness communicates presumption.

God entrusts more only after trust has been proven.

REFLECTIVE SUMMARY

This chapter has emphasized that faithfulness in the early stages of ministry is inward before it is outward. God examines how His servants steward their calling, motives, integrity, and obedience long before they are entrusted with greater responsibility.

Stewardship at this level is about guarding the call, not managing others.

Scripture shows that **faithfulness in small, unseen matters prepares the minister for future trust.** Integrity, patience, and reverence formed early become safeguards later.

Those who honor the calling in its formative stage position themselves to carry it responsibly in seasons yet to come.

CLOSING CHARGE

Guard the calling God has placed upon your life.

Be faithful with your time, your obedience, and your private walk with Him. Do not despise small beginnings or unseen seasons.

What God is forming in you now is preparing you for what He will entrust to you later.

Resist the urge to rush, compare, or seek recognition. Faithfulness in this season is shaping your character and protecting your future.

Carry the calling with reverence, patience, and humility, knowing that God watches how you steward what He has already given.

If you are not faithful now, you will not be ready later.

REFLECTIVE QUESTIONS

1. How am I stewarding the calling God has placed upon my life right now?

2. Are there areas where impatience or ambition threatens my faithfulness?

3. How consistent is my obedience in unseen or ordinary responsibilities?

4. What motives does the Holy Ghost need to refine in me during this season?

5. How can I better guard the calling entrusted to me?

PRAYER

Father, teach me to be faithful with what You have placed in my hands. Guard my heart from impatience, ambition, and carelessness.

Help me to honor the calling in its formative stage and to walk in obedience, integrity, and humility.

Prepare me for what is ahead by shaping me faithfully where I am.

In Jesus' Name, Amen.

CHAPTER 6

GUARDING DOCTRINE, TRUTH, AND THE INTEGRITY OF THE GOSPEL

Truth is not optional in ministry—it is the foundation.

Before a minister is entrusted to proclaim truth publicly, he must first be formed privately by that truth.

Doctrine is not merely what a minister teaches—it is what governs how a minister lives, thinks, and responds.

Paul wrote to the Romans, *"Be not conformed to this world: but be ye transformed by the renewing of your mind"* **(Romans 12:2).**

Transformation begins internally. A minister's mind must be shaped by truth before his mouth can faithfully declare it.

When doctrine is neglected or distorted, ministry becomes opinion-driven rather than Spirit-led.

A minister who mishandles truth will eventually mislead people.

DOCTRINE AS FORMATION, NOT ARGUMENT

In **Volume 1,** doctrine must be understood primarily as formation, not debate.

The minister is not yet being trained to win arguments—but to be governed by truth.

Paul warned the Galatians that beginning in the Spirit and attempting to mature in the flesh leads to corruption (Galatians 3:3).

Wrong doctrine always produces wrong direction.

Sound doctrine:

- shapes humility

- produces reverence

- guards against deception

- stabilizes the mind

- anchors obedience

- protects against pride

Paul reminded the Ephesians that immature believers are *"tossed to and fro" by every wind of doctrine* **(Ephesians 4:14).**

Stability comes from truth internalized, not merely memorized.

THE GOSPEL MUST REMAIN CENTRAL

Paul declared to the Corinthians, *"I determined not to know any thing among you, save Jesus Christ, and him crucified"* **(1 Corinthians 2:2).**

The minister must guard against drifting away from the simplicity and power of the Gospel.

When personality, performance, or philosophy replaces Christ, doctrine is already compromised.

The Gospel:

- humbles the minister
- centers Christ
- exposes pride
- confronts sin
- reveals grace
- produces obedience

Paul warned that even angels preaching a different gospel must be rejected **(Galatians 1:8).**

The Gospel does not change with culture, pressure, or preference.

WHEN TRUTH IS INCONVENIENT

Truth will not always be easy to preach, and it will not always be easy to live.

There will be moments when truth:

- confronts culture
- challenges relationships
- exposes sin
- costs acceptance

A minister must decide early: will I adjust truth to fit people, or will I stand on truth and trust God?

Compromised truth may gain approval—but it loses power.

Faithful truth may cost something—but it carries authority.

TRUTH LIVED BEFORE TRUTH TAUGHT

Doctrine must be lived before it is taught.

Paul told the Philippians, *"Those things, which ye have both learned, and received, and heard, and seen in me, do"* **(Philippians 4:9).**

Truth carried inconsistently loses authority.

The minister must allow Scripture to govern:

- conduct
- speech
- attitudes
- decisions

Colossians instructs, *"Let the word of Christ dwell in you richly"* **(Colossians 3:16).**

Doctrine that merely visits the mind will not sustain the heart. Only truth that dwells produces endurance and consistency.

GUARDING AGAINST SUBTLE DRIFT

Paul warned the Thessalonians to *"prove all things; hold fast that which is good"* **(1 Thessalonians 5:21).**

Not all error appears blatant—some drift begins subtly.

Drift is dangerous because it is rarely noticed when it begins.

It often begins with:

- small compromises
- softened language
- neglected Scripture
- selective obedience
- prioritizing acceptance over truth

What is tolerated in small measure will grow if left uncorrected.

The minister must cultivate discernment early.

Doctrine guards the soul before it guards the pulpit.

DOCTRINE AND THE HOLY GHOST

Truth is not grasped by intellect alone.

Paul wrote, *"Which things also we speak, not in the words which man's wisdom teacheth, but which the Holy Ghost teacheth"* **(1 Corinthians 2:13).**

Doctrine separated from the Spirit becomes cold and rigid; spirituality separated from doctrine becomes unstable.

The Spirit will never lead contrary to the Word, and the Word will never contradict the Spirit.

The Holy Ghost:

- illuminates truth

- convicts error

- applies Scripture

- guards interpretation

- keeps doctrine alive

A minister must submit both mind and spirit to the authority of God's Word.

SUFFERING FOR TRUTH

Paul reminded Timothy—and all ministers—that standing for truth carries a cost.

He testified, *"We are troubled on every side, yet not distressed... cast down, but not destroyed"* **(2 Corinthians 4:8–9).**

Ministers who refuse to compromise doctrine will face resistance, misunderstanding, and sometimes rejection.

If you stand for truth long enough, you will be tested for it.

In **Volume 1**, the minister must accept this reality early:

Faithfulness to truth may be costly—but compromise is always more expensive.

REFLECTIVE SUMMARY

This chapter has emphasized that **doctrine is formative before it is declarative.** Sound teaching renews the mind, stabilizes the heart, and guards the minister against deception and drift.

The Gospel must remain central, and truth must be lived before it is taught.

Doctrine that is not lived loses power, and spirituality that is not grounded in truth loses direction.

Ministers formed by sound doctrine become anchored, discerning, and consistent.

Guarding truth in the inner life prepares the servant to proclaim it faithfully in seasons yet to come.

CLOSING CHARGE

Guard the truth that has been entrusted to you.

Do not treat Scripture casually, selectively, or lightly.

What you tolerate in your inner life today will shape what you proclaim tomorrow.

Resist the temptation to soften truth for comfort, approval, or acceptance.

Let Christ remain central. Let the Gospel remain pure. Let the Word remain authoritative.

Commit yourself to truth lived quietly, consistently, and reverently.

God entrusts His message only to those who submit fully to its power.

Truth is not yours to adjust—it is yours to uphold.

REFLECTIVE QUESTIONS

1. How deeply does Scripture shape my thinking and daily decisions?

2. Are there truths I accept intellectually but resist practically?

3. How do I guard against subtle doctrinal drift in my life?

4. Is Christ and the Gospel central in my understanding of ministry?

5. How dependent am I on the Holy Ghost to teach and apply truth?

PRAYER

Lord, root me deeply in Your truth. Renew my mind, guard my heart, and keep me anchored in the Gospel.

Protect me from error, compromise, and drift.

Teach me by Your Spirit and help me to live what I believe.

Let Your Word dwell richly within me and prepare me to carry truth faithfully.

In Jesus' Name, Amen.

CHAPTER 7

ENDURANCE, PATIENCE, AND HIDDEN SEASONS OF PREPARATION

God does His deepest work in seasons no one else can see.

What God prepares in secret, He reveals in time.

Every calling from God includes seasons that are unseen, misunderstood, and often uncomfortable. These hidden seasons are not delays—they are divine appointments.

God forms His servants in obscurity before He entrusts them with visibility.

Endurance and patience are not optional virtues in ministry—they are essential disciplines that protect the calling and preserve the servant.

Paul wrote, *"Tribulation worketh patience; and patience, experience; and experience, hope"* **(Romans 5:3–4).**

Pressure is not punishment—it is preparation.

The minister who resists hidden seasons often resists the very process God is using to prepare them.

WHY GOD USES HIDDEN SEASONS

Hidden seasons strip away self-reliance and expose motives.

When no one is watching, applauding, or affirming, the minister discovers whether obedience is rooted in love for God or desire for recognition.

Hidden seasons reveal who you are without an audience.

Paul reminded the Galatians, *"Let us not be weary in well doing: for in due season we shall reap, if we faint not"* **(Galatians 6:9).**

Due season belongs to God—not to man.

In hidden seasons, God teaches His servants to:

- wait without complaining
- pray without visible results
- obey without immediate reward

Patience is not passivity—it is active trust in God's timing.

ENDURANCE AS A SPIRITUAL DISCIPLINE

Endurance is the ability to remain faithful under pressure without hardening the heart.

Paul told the Corinthians that ministers are often *"troubled on every side, yet not distressed; perplexed, but not in despair"* **(2 Corinthians 4:8).**

Endurance is staying where God placed you, even when it is uncomfortable.

Endurance develops:

- **Spiritual resilience** — remaining anchored in truth when circumstances challenge faith

- **Emotional steadiness** — responding rather than reacting under pressure

- **Mental discipline** — guarding thoughts against discouragement and comparison

- **Moral consistency** — refusing to compromise under pressure

- **Dependence on grace** — recognizing strength comes from God, not self

These qualities cannot be rushed.

They are formed through repeated obedience in difficult conditions.

Many fall away not because they lacked gifting—but because they lacked endurance.

Endurance safeguards the calling until fulfillment arrives.

THE TEST OF WAITING

Waiting is one of God's primary tools of preparation.

It exposes impatience, confronts expectations, and reveals whether trust is genuine.

Waiting reveals what you truly believe about God.

A minister must learn to wait without becoming frustrated, bitter, or distracted.

Waiting tests:

- Motives
- Priorities
- Faith
- submission

God often delays what He has promised—not to deny it, but to prepare the one who will carry it.

If you cannot wait with God, you cannot walk with God.

THE TEMPTATION TO QUIT

Every hidden season carries a quiet temptation—to quit.

To walk away.

To stop praying.

To settle for less than what God promised.

Frustration whispers that nothing is happening.

Delay suggests that nothing will change.

But quitting in the process forfeits what endurance would have produced.

Many do not fail because God did not call them—they fail because they did not endure long enough.

HIDDENNESS AND IDENTITY

Hidden seasons protect identity.

When a minister is unseen, they are protected from premature exposure, pride, and pressure.

God hides His servants so they can be formed without distraction.

In hiddenness:

- **identity** is secured in God—not in recognition

- **confidence** is built in truth—not in applause

- **character** is strengthened without public pressure

If identity is built on visibility, it will collapse under pressure.

THE DANGER OF RESISTING THE PROCESS

Not every minister fails because of sin—many fail because they resist preparation.

They rush ahead of God's timing.

They seek visibility before stability.

They desire influence without formation.

Impatience has caused many to step out of the will of God prematurely.

What is obtained prematurely cannot be sustained properly.

You can delay what God intends to develop if you refuse the process.

When preparation is resisted:

- pride increases

- instability develops

- pressure overwhelms

- compromise becomes more likely

God prepares before He promotes. Always.

WHEN GOD SEEMS SILENT

There are seasons when God feels silent.

Prayers seem unanswered.

Direction feels unclear.

Progress appears slow.

But silence does not mean absence.

God is often most active when He appears most silent.

God's silence is never empty—it is always purposeful.

In these moments, the minister must:

- remain faithful

- continue obeying

- trust what God has already spoken

Silence is not rejection—it is often refinement.

THE REWARD OF ENDURANCE

Those who endure are strengthened, stabilized, and prepared.

James wrote, *"Blessed is the man that endureth temptation: for when he is tried, he shall receive the crown of life"* **(James 1:12).**

Endurance produces:

- spiritual depth
- emotional strength
- clarity of calling
- confidence in God

What endurance builds cannot be shaken easily.

REFLECTIVE SUMMARY

This chapter has emphasized that **hidden seasons are not delays—they are part of God's preparation process.** Endurance and patience are developed through pressure, waiting, and unseen obedience.

God uses these seasons to refine motives, strengthen character, and establish stability.

Endurance is not simply surviving difficulty— it is remaining faithful through it.

Ministers who embrace hidden seasons are prepared to carry public responsibility without collapsing under pressure.

What God builds in obscurity, He can trust in visibility.

CLOSING CHARGE

Do not despise the hidden seasons of your life.

Do not rush what God is still forming.

Remain faithful when unseen. Remain obedient when it is difficult. Remain patient when progress feels slow.

What God is doing in you now is preparing you for what He will do through you later.

Trust His timing. Submit to His process. Endure without complaint.

If you quit in hiddenness, you will never stand in visibility.

What you become in hiddenness will determine what you can carry in visibility.

REFLECTIVE QUESTIONS

1. How do I respond when God places me in a hidden or waiting season?

2. Are there areas where impatience is causing me to resist God's process?

3. What is God developing in me during this current season?

4. How do I handle pressure, silence, or lack of recognition?

5. Am I willing to remain faithful even when no one sees or acknowledges it?

PRAYER

Lord, teach me to endure with faith and patience. Help me to trust Your timing and submit to Your process.

Strengthen me in hidden seasons and guard my heart from frustration, impatience, and discouragement.

Develop in me the character, stability, and endurance required to carry what You have called me to do.

Let me remain faithful, even when unseen.

In Jesus' Name, Amen.

CHAPTER 8

FAITHFULNESS BEFORE FUNCTION

God is not looking for availability alone—He is looking for reliability.

God is not in a hurry to use you—He is committed to preparing you.

One of the greatest misunderstandings in ministry is the belief that calling immediately requires function. Many feel the call of God and assume that they must quickly move into visible roles, public ministry, or positions of influence.

But Scripture consistently reveals a different pattern.

God establishes faithfulness before He assigns function.

Before **David** wore a crown, he tended sheep.

Before **Joseph** governed Egypt, he served in prison.

Before **the disciples** preached publicly, they followed privately.

Function without faithfulness produces instability.

THE DANGER OF MOVING TOO QUICKLY

Many ministers struggle because they move into function before they are formed.

They preach before they are grounded.

They lead before they are disciplined.

They speak before they have learned to listen.

What begins prematurely often collapses unnecessarily.

God does not rush preparation, even when man desires acceleration.

When function comes before faithfulness:

- character is underdeveloped

- motives remain unchecked

- pressure exposes weakness

- responsibility overwhelms

Premature exposure creates unnecessary failure.

THE PRESSURE TO BE SEEN

Many struggle in this season not because they lack calling—but because they feel overlooked.

They see others moving ahead.

They see opportunities passing by.

They feel ready—but remain unseen.

This pressure can lead to striving, comparison, and self-promotion.

But what God withholds in one season is often what He is protecting.

Visibility without preparation leads to exposure without stability.

FAITHFULNESS IN SMALL ASSIGNMENTS

Jesus said, *"He that is faithful in that which is least is faithful also in much"* **(Luke 16:10).**

Faithfulness is proven in small, unseen responsibilities long before it is demonstrated in public ministry.

This includes:

- consistency in prayer

- seriousness in studying the Word

- obedience in daily life

- reliability in commitments

- humility in service

God watches how you handle what seems insignificant.

Small assignments are not meaningless—they are **training grounds.**

How you treat small responsibilities reveals how you will handle greater ones.

How you serve in private determines how you will stand in public.

SERVING BEFORE LEADING

Before a minister is called to lead, they must learn to serve.

Jesus said, *"Whosoever will be chief among you, let him be your servant"* **(Matthew 20:27).**

Ministry begins with servanthood—not position.

Serving develops:

- humility
- patience
- compassion
- understanding of people

Serving reveals whether you want the work—or the recognition.

A minister who refuses to serve will eventually struggle to lead.

Those who cannot follow instructions will not handle authority well.

THE FORMATION OF CHARACTER BEFORE FUNCTION

God is far more concerned with character than with gifting.

Gifts may open doors—but character determines how long you remain.

Function reveals what is already formed—nothing more.

If character has not been developed:

- pride will surface

- pressure will expose weakness

- decisions will lack wisdom

- relationships will suffer

Character is what sustains what calling begins.

THE TEST OF CONSISTENCY

Faithfulness is not proven in moments—it is proven over time.

Consistency in unseen seasons reveals maturity.

Anyone can be faithful occasionally—but God looks for those who are faithful consistently.

Consistency includes:

- obeying when it is inconvenient
- remaining steady when emotions fluctuate
- continuing when progress is slow
- showing up when no one notices

Consistency is the evidence that your faith is real, not seasonal.

Consistency builds trust—with God and with people.

WHEN FUNCTION IS DELAYED

There are seasons when God delays visible function.

This delay is not denial—it is preparation.

God delays exposure to protect what He is developing.

During these seasons, the minister must resist:

- frustration
- comparison
- impatience
- self-promotion

Many have lost their way by pursuing position instead of preparation.

If you promote yourself, you may bypass what God is trying to build.

God knows when you are ready—far better than you do.

THE DANGER OF IDENTITY IN FUNCTION

One of the greatest dangers in ministry is finding identity in what you do rather than who you are in God.

If your identity is rooted in function, you will struggle when function changes.

If function defines you, its absence will break you.

Titles can change.

Opportunities can shift.

Platforms can come and go.

But identity must remain rooted in Christ.

You are not your function—you are God's servant.

FUNCTION WILL COME IN ITS TIME

God is not withholding purpose—He is preparing the vessel.

When faithfulness is established and character is formed, function will come naturally.

What God releases in His timing will not require striving to sustain.

You will not have to force doors open.

You will not have to fight for recognition.

You will not have to prove yourself.

What God gives, He sustains—what you force, you must maintain.

God opens what no man can shut.

REFLECTIVE SUMMARY

This chapter has emphasized that **faithfulness must come before function.** God prepares His servants through small responsibilities, hidden service, and consistent obedience before entrusting them with greater assignments.

Rushing into function without formation leads to instability, while faithful preparation produces endurance and strength.

Character, consistency, and humility are developed long before visibility is granted.

Ministers who embrace faithfulness in unseen seasons position themselves to function effectively without compromising their calling.

CLOSING CHARGE

Do not chase function—pursue faithfulness.

Do not rush what God is still forming in you.

Be faithful in small things. Serve with humility. Remain consistent in private.

What God is preparing in you is more important than what He is doing through you right now.

Trust His process. Submit to His timing. Resist the urge to promote yourself.

If you are faithful where you are, God will position you where you need to be.

Faithfulness is not a stage—it is a lifestyle.

REFLECTIVE QUESTIONS

1. Am I focused more on function than on faithfulness?

2. How do I respond when my opportunities seem limited or delayed?

3. In what areas is God calling me to be more consistent?

4. Am I willing to serve faithfully without recognition?

5. Is my identity rooted in Christ or in what I do?

PRAYER

Lord, teach me to be faithful before I seek to function. Help me to embrace the process of preparation and to serve with humility and consistency.

Guard my heart from impatience, comparison, and self-promotion.

Develop my character, strengthen my discipline, and establish my identity in You.

Prepare me fully before You release me.

In Jesus' Name, Amen.

CHAPTER 9

WHEN THE CALL CONFRONTS

God will confront in you what He plans to correct through you.

The call of God will not leave you as it found you.

Many enter ministry expecting affirmation, direction, and purpose. And while God does provide those things, He also does something many do not anticipate: **He confronts.**

The call of God confronts:

- Sin
- Motives
- Character
- Priorities
- Identity

Before God uses you publicly, He will deal with you privately.

THE CALL EXPOSES WHAT IS HIDDEN

When God calls you, He begins to reveal what has been buried, ignored, or excused.

Things you once overlooked suddenly become clear.

Convictions grow stronger.

Compromise becomes harder to tolerate.

The call of God brings light—and light exposes everything.

Scripture declares, *"For there is nothing covered, that shall not be revealed"* **(Luke 12:2).**

God does not expose to shame—He exposes to cleanse.

What God reveals, He intends to heal.

CONFRONTING PERSONAL SIN AND WEAKNESS

No one answers the call of God perfectly formed.

There are weaknesses.

There are struggles.

There are areas of immaturity.

God will deal with these areas directly.

He will:

- correct attitudes
- challenge behaviors
- convict your heart
- demand repentance

What you refuse to confront, God will not ignore.

God will not anoint what He has not first addressed.

Avoiding correction limits growth.

Embracing correction produces transformation.

THE CONFRONTATION OF MOTIVES

Why do you want to be used by God?

This is a question you must answer honestly.

God examines:

- ambition
- desire for recognition
- need for validation
- hidden pride

God is not only concerned with what you do—but why you do it.

You can do the right thing for the wrong reason—and God will still confront it.

Impure motives will eventually corrupt pure assignments.

WHEN GOD CORRECTS YOU

Correction is one of the clearest signs that God is working in your life.

Scripture says, *"For whom the Lord loveth he chasteneth"* **(Hebrews 12:6).**

Yet correction often meets resistance.

You may feel defensive.

You may want to justify yourself.

You may resist what is being revealed.

But correction is not rejection—it is refinement.

God corrects:

- through His Word
- through the Holy Ghost
- through circumstances
- through godly leadership

If you cannot receive correction, you cannot be trusted with responsibility.

THE STRUGGLE WITH CORRECTION

Correction challenges how you see yourself.

It exposes what you would rather ignore.

It confronts what you have justified.

It calls you higher than you are currently living.

Many struggle not because they do not hear God—but because they do not want to change.

Pride resists correction.

Humility receives it.

Growth begins where resistance ends.

THE CALL WILL DISRUPT YOUR COMFORT

The call of God will interrupt your plans.

It will challenge your comfort.

It will confront your preferences.

It will stretch your faith.

Comfort is often the greatest enemy of calling.

God does not call you to convenience—He calls you to obedience.

What once felt normal may no longer feel acceptable.

What once satisfied you may no longer be enough.

The call requires change.

WHEN OBEDIENCE IS UNCOMFORTABLE

There will be moments when obedience is difficult.

God may ask you to:

- walk away from relationships

- release opportunities

- remain silent when you want to speak

- step forward when you feel unready

Obedience is not always easy—but it is always necessary.

Partial obedience is still disobedience.

Delayed obedience is still disobedience.

God honors complete obedience.

THE COST OF IGNORING CONFRONTATION

You can hear God—and still resist what He reveals.

You can continue patterns.

You can ignore conviction.

You can delay change.

What is ignored will not disappear—it will grow.

Uncorrected areas today become public failures tomorrow.

Ignoring confrontation leads to:

- spiritual stagnation
- weakened discernment
- compromised integrity
- limited effectiveness

Delay in obedience increases consequence.

God will not build on what you refuse to surrender.

THE BLESSING OF SUBMISSION

Those who submit to God's correction are strengthened, not diminished.

Submission produces:

- clarity

- freedom

- maturity

- stability

Submission positions you for transformation.

What God removes, He replaces with something better.

Submission is not weakness—it is alignment.

Brokenness before God produces strength in ministry.

WHEN THE CALL CHANGES YOU

You cannot answer the call of God and remain the same.

Your thinking will change.

Your priorities will shift.

Your desires will be refined.

The call is not just about what you do—it is about who you become.

God is not only preparing your assignment—He is preparing you.

REFLECTIVE SUMMARY

This chapter has emphasized that **the call of God confronts before it commissions.** God exposes sin, challenges motives, and corrects behavior to prepare His servants for effective ministry.

Confrontation is not rejection—it is transformation.

What God reveals, He intends to refine.

Those who embrace correction, surrender their motives, and walk in obedience are strengthened and prepared for greater responsibility.

CLOSING CHARGE

Do not resist what God is revealing in your life.

Do not ignore conviction. Do not delay obedience.

Allow God to confront, correct, and refine you.

What you surrender now will strengthen what you carry later.

Choose obedience over comfort. Choose submission over resistance.

God cannot use what you refuse to yield.

What you allow God to correct now will determine what He can trust you with later.

REFLECTIVE QUESTIONS

1. What areas of my life is God currently confronting or correcting?

2. How do I respond when I feel conviction or correction?

3. Are there motives that need to be purified in my heart?

4. What am I resisting that God is asking me to surrender?

5. Am I willing to change in order to grow into my calling?

PRAYER

Lord, search my heart and reveal anything in me that is not aligned with Your will.

Help me to receive correction with humility and to respond with obedience.

Purify my motives, strengthen my character, and refine my life.

Teach me to surrender fully so that I may be prepared for what You have called me to do.

In Jesus' Name, Amen.

CHAPTER 10

THE MINISTER WITHIN THE BODY: SERVING WITHOUT POSITION

No minister is called to stand alone—every minister is called to function within the Body.

The call of God is personal, but it is never independent.

Many misunderstand this and begin to view their calling as something separate from the church, leadership, or spiritual authority. But Scripture reveals a different pattern.

God places His servants within a Body—not outside of it.

Paul wrote, *"Now ye are the body of Christ, and members in particular"* **(1 Corinthians 12:27).**

A calling disconnected from the Body becomes unstable.

GOD ESTABLISHES ORDER IN THE BODY

God is a God of order.

He sets structure, leadership, and accountability within His church.

Paul wrote, *"Let all things be done decently and in order"* **(1 Corinthians 14:40).**

Order is not restriction—it is protection.

Within the Body, God establishes:

- Leadership
- Accountability
- Covering
- Guidance
- correction

Spiritual order protects both the minister and the ministry.

THE DANGER OF INDEPENDENT MINISTRY

One of the greatest dangers in early ministry is independence.

Some feel called and immediately begin to separate themselves from authority.

Others resist correction or avoid accountability.

Independence in ministry is not strength—it is vulnerability.

Independence often feels spiritual—but it is usually rooted in pride.

When a minister operates independently:

- accountability is lost

- correction is resisted

- pride increases

- error goes unchecked

What is not submitted cannot be properly sustained.

Many have damaged their calling by refusing to stay submitted.

SUBMISSION TO SPIRITUAL AUTHORITY

Submission is a foundational principle in the Body of Christ.

Scripture teaches, *"Obey them that have the rule over you, and submit yourselves"* **(Hebrews 13:17).**

Submission is not weakness—it is alignment with God's structure.

Submission includes:

- receiving instruction
- accepting correction
- honoring leadership
- remaining teachable

You cannot be trusted with authority if you resist being under authority.

THE STRUGGLE WITH SUBMISSION

Submission is often resisted not because it is unclear—but because it is uncomfortable.

It challenges pride.

It confronts independence.

It requires trust.

Many want to be used by God—but struggle to be led by others.

Submission exposes whether you truly trust God's order or prefer your own control.

Where submission is resisted, growth is limited.

HONORING THOSE GOD HAS PLACED OVER YOU

Honor is essential in ministry.

Paul instructed believers to esteem leaders highly for their work's sake **(1 Thessalonians 5:12–13).**

Honor reflects your understanding of God's order.

How you treat authority reveals how you view God's structure.

Dishonor often begins subtly:

- questioning authority
- resisting instruction
- speaking critically
- withholding respect

A dishonoring spirit will eventually hinder your growth.

UNITY WITHIN THE BODY

God does not call ministers to compete—but to function together.

Paul wrote that the Body is *"fitly joined together"* **(Ephesians 4:16).**

Unity is not uniformity—it is cooperation under God's design.

Within the Body:

- each member has a role

- each function is necessary

- each calling contributes

You cannot walk in unity if you are constantly measuring yourself against others.

Division weakens what unity strengthens.

THE ROLE OF ACCOUNTABILITY

Accountability protects the minister from error and drift.

It provides:

- **correction** when needed

- **guidance** in decision-making

- **protection** from blind spots

- **spiritual covering**

Those who reject accountability often expose themselves to unnecessary failure.

Accountability is not control—it is care.

SERVING WITHIN YOUR ASSIGNED PLACE

God assigns each minister a place within the Body.

Not every role is visible.

Not every assignment is public.

Not every calling is the same.

Faithfulness in your assigned place is more important than visibility in another.

Comparison leads to frustration.

Submission leads to growth.

Stay where God has placed you until He moves you.

Leaving your place prematurely can delay your development unnecessarily.

THE DANGER OF COMPARISON AND COMPETITION

Comparison is destructive in ministry.

It leads to:

- jealousy
- insecurity
- striving
- dissatisfaction

When you compare your calling to others, you lose focus on what God has given you.

Competition has no place in the Body.

You are not called to outdo others—you are called to obey God.

GROWING WITHIN THE BODY

Growth in ministry does not happen in isolation.

It happens:

- under leadership
- through correction
- within community
- through service

God uses people to shape people.

Isolation limits growth.

Connection strengthens it.

WHEN GOD BEGINS TO ELEVATE YOU

There will be a time when God increases responsibility.

But elevation must come through God's timing—not self-promotion.

What God establishes, He sustains.

As responsibility increases:

- humility must increase

- submission must remain

- honor must continue

If you rise without submission, you will struggle to remain where you have been placed.

How you rise matters just as much as when you rise.

REFLECTIVE SUMMARY

This chapter has emphasized that **the minister is called to function within the Body of Christ, not apart from it.** God establishes order, authority, and accountability to protect both the servant and the calling.

Submission, honor, unity, and accountability are essential for healthy ministry.

Independence leads to instability, but alignment produces growth and strength.

Ministers who embrace their place within the Body position themselves for long-term effectiveness and stability.

CLOSING CHARGE

Do not separate yourself from the Body God has placed you in.

Embrace order. Honor leadership. Submit to authority.

Serve faithfully where you are, without comparison or competition.

What God is building in you will be strengthened through the people He has placed around you.

Stay connected. Stay submitted. Stay teachable.

God does not raise independent ministers—He raises submitted servants.

Your connection to the Body will determine your stability in ministry.

REFLECTIVE QUESTIONS

1. Am I fully submitted to the spiritual authority God has placed in my life?

2. How do I respond to correction, instruction, and accountability?

3. Am I comparing my calling to others instead of embracing my assignment?

4. What role has God given me within the Body right now?

5. Am I committed to unity, or do I struggle with independence?

PRAYER

Lord, help me to walk in humility, submission, and unity within the Body of Christ.

Teach me to honor those You have placed over me and to remain teachable in every season.

Guard my heart from pride, comparison, and independence.

Help me to serve faithfully where You have placed me and to grow within the structure You have established.

In Jesus' Name, Amen.

CHAPTER 11

TESTED, PROVEN, AND ENTRUSTED

God does not entrust potential—He entrusts proven character.

God does not entrust what has not been tested.

Every minister desire to be used by God. But before God entrusts greater responsibility, He allows seasons of testing, proving, and preparation.

Calling introduces you—testing reveals you.

Many are called.

Fewer are proven.

Even fewer are entrusted.

THE PURPOSE OF TESTING

Testing is not designed to destroy you—it is designed to reveal you.

God tests:

- your obedience

- your motives

- your consistency

- your character

- your response under pressure

Testing exposes what is genuine and what is not.

Scripture declares, *"The Lord trieth the righteous"* **(Psalm 11:5).**

What is untested cannot be trusted.

TESTED IN PRIVATE BEFORE TRUSTED IN PUBLIC

God's pattern is consistent:

He tests in private before He entrusts in public.

Before **David** was king, he was tested in the field.

Before **Joseph** ruled, he was tested in hardship.

Before **the apostles** led, they were tested in following.

What is developed in secret determines what can be sustained in public.

Private victories produce public stability.

THE PROVING PROCESS

Proving is the continuation of testing over time.

It is not one moment—it is a pattern.

Proven character is consistent character.

A proven minister:

- obeys when it is difficult
- remains faithful when unnoticed
- stays humble when growing
- responds correctly under pressure

God looks for patterns, not moments.

Anyone can be faithful occasionally.

God entrusts those who are faithful consistently.

WHEN TRUST IS GIVEN

There comes a point where God begins to entrust more.

More responsibility.

More influence.

More visibility.

But this is not a reward—it is a responsibility.

What God entrusts must be handled with reverence.

Trust includes:

- stewarding people wisely

- handling influence carefully

- maintaining integrity consistently

- remaining dependent on God

What you prayed for now requires discipline to sustain.

THE TEST OF TRUST

Being entrusted is not the end of testing—it is a new level of testing.

Now your decisions carry weight.

Your words influence others.

Your actions affect more than just you.

What you do with what God has given you becomes a test of trust.

Will you remain humble?

Will you stay dependent?

Will you guard what has been placed in your hands?

Many handle testing well—but fail when trust is given.

THE WEIGHT OF RESPONSIBILITY

With greater trust comes greater weight.

Responsibility is not always easy—it is often heavy.

The weight of ministry will expose what has not been developed.

Responsibility reveals whether you were truly prepared or merely promoted.

Without preparation:

- pressure overwhelms

- decisions become careless

- pride begins to grow

- dependence on God weakens

What you carry must be supported by who you have become.

STAYING HUMBLE WHEN ELEVATED

One of the greatest dangers after being entrusted is pride.

Recognition increases.

Influence grows.

Opportunities expand.

But elevation tests humility just as much as obscurity tests faithfulness.

Pride does not always announce itself—it often grows quietly after elevation.

A minister must remember:

- you are still dependent on God

- you are still accountable

- you are still being formed

What you become after elevation matters as much as what you were before it.

GUARDING WHAT HAS BEEN ENTRUSTED

What God entrusts must be guarded.

Paul told Timothy to *"keep that which is committed to thy trust"* **(1 Timothy 6:20).**

This requires:

- vigilance

- discipline

- prayer

- self-awareness

What is not guarded can be lost.

Neglect is just as dangerous as rebellion.

What you fail to manage well can be taken from you.

Many do not fail in calling—they fail in stewardship after being entrusted.

THE CONTINUED NEED FOR DEPENDENCE

Entrustment does not eliminate dependence—it increases it.

The more God gives, the more you must rely on Him.

You never outgrow your need for God.

Prayer must remain.

Submission must remain.

Discipline must remain.

The level you reach will expose the level you rely on God.

The same principles that prepared you must sustain you.

FINISHING WELL

The goal is not just to begin—it is to finish.

Paul declared, *"I have fought a good fight, I have finished my course, I have kept the faith"* **(2 Timothy 4:7).**

Starting strong is important—but finishing well is essential.

Many start with passion—but only a few finish with faithfulness.

Finishing well requires:

- endurance
- faithfulness
- humility
- consistency

What you do over time matters more than what you do in moments.

REFLECTIVE SUMMARY

This chapter has emphasized that **God tests, proves,** and **then entrusts**. Testing reveals character, proving establishes consistency, and entrustment brings responsibility.

What is developed in private becomes visible in public, and what is proven over time becomes trusted.

Entrustment is not a reward—it is a responsibility that must be carried with humility and care.

Ministers who remain dependent on God, guard what has been entrusted, and continue in faithfulness position themselves to finish well.

CLOSING CHARGE

Do not seek to be entrusted—seek to be proven.

Allow God to test you, refine you, and establish you.

When God entrusts you with more, carry it with humility, discipline, and reverence.

What you have prayed for will require you to grow in order to sustain it.

Stay dependent on God. Stay faithful. Stay humble.

What God entrusts to you must be guarded, honored, and carried well.

How you handle what God entrusts will determine what He entrusts next.

REFLECTIVE QUESTIONS

1. How do I respond when I am being tested or stretched?

2. What patterns in my life reveal consistency—or inconsistency?

3. Am I prepared to handle greater responsibility with humility?

4. How am I guarding what God has already entrusted to me?

5. Am I living in a way that will allow me to finish well?

PRAYER

Lord, prepare me through every test and establish me through every season of proving.

Help me to remain faithful, consistent, and humble as You develop my life.

Teach me to carry responsibility with reverence and to guard what You entrust to me.

Strengthen me to remain dependent on You so that I may finish well.

In Jesus' Name, Amen.

CHAPTER 12

REMAIN FAITHFUL: THE FINAL CHARGE

The calling of God is not proven in how you begin—but in how you remain.

You have been called.

You have been taught.

You have been prepared.

Now comes the responsibility:

Remain faithful.

Many begin with excitement.

Many respond to the call with sincerity.

But over time, challenges arise.

Pressure increases.

Opportunities shift.

The true test of calling is not beginning—it is continuing.

THE CALL TO REMAIN

Paul wrote, *"Moreover it is required in stewards, that a man be found faithful"* **(1 Corinthians 4:2).**

Faithfulness is not a moment—it is a lifelong commitment.

It is not proven in seasons of ease, but in seasons of difficulty.

Remaining requires intentionality.

You must choose:

- obedience when it is inconvenient
- discipline when it is difficult
- humility when you are recognized
- consistency when you are tired

Remaining is a decision made daily.

WHEN THE JOURNEY BECOMES DIFFICULT

There will be seasons when the journey feels heavy.

You may experience:

- discouragement

- misunderstanding

- opposition

- weariness

These moments are not signs to stop—they are opportunities to remain.

Many abandon their calling not because God failed—but because they became weary.

Paul warned, *"Let us not be weary in well doing..."* **(Galatians 6:9).**

Weariness is real—but it must not become a reason to quit.

GUARDING YOUR WALK WITH GOD

Everything in your calling flows from your relationship with God.

If that weakens, everything else becomes unstable.

You must guard your walk with God above everything else.

This requires:

- consistent prayer
- continual engagement with Scripture
- sensitivity to the Holy Ghost
- regular self-examination

What is neglected privately will eventually affect you publicly.

STAYING GROUNDED IN TRUTH

Doctrine must remain your foundation.

As time passes, there will be pressure to adjust, soften, or compromise.

Truth must remain unchanging—even when culture shifts.

You must:

- hold firmly to Scripture

- resist compromise

- remain anchored in the Gospel

What you stand on determines how you stand.

REMAINING HUMBLE

No matter how far God brings you, humility must remain.

Pride is subtle.

It grows quietly.

It often appears after progress.

What you have received is by grace—not by your own strength.

Humility keeps you:

- teachable
- dependent
- grounded

What pride builds, God resists. What humility carries, God sustains.

STAYING CONNECTED TO THE BODY

You are not called to walk alone.

You must remain connected:

- to the Body of Christ

- to spiritual authority

- to accountability

Isolation weakens. Connection strengthens.

The same principles that guided you at the beginning must remain with you as you continue.

FINISHING YOUR COURSE

Paul declared, *"I have finished my course, I have kept the faith"* **(2 Timothy 4:7).**

This must be your goal.

Not just to begin.

Not just to grow.

But to finish.

Finishing requires endurance, faithfulness, and consistency over time.

Some will start strong and fade.

Others will endure and finish.

Determine now which one you will be.

THE LEGACY OF A FAITHFUL LIFE

Your calling is not only about you—it is about what remains after you.

A faithful life produces:

- lasting impact

- spiritual fruit

- influence that continues

Faithfulness leaves a legacy that extends beyond your lifetime.

What you build in obedience will outlast you.

THE FINAL DECISION

At the end of all teaching, preparation, and instruction, one question remains:

Will you remain faithful?

No one can answer that for you.

It will be decided:

- in your daily choices
- in your private life
- in your response to difficulty
- in your commitment to obedience

Faithfulness is not automatic—it is intentional.

REFLECTIVE SUMMARY

This chapter has emphasized that **the ultimate responsibility of the called life is to remain faithful.** Faithfulness is demonstrated through consistency, humility, obedience, and endurance over time.

The challenges of ministry do not remove the calling—they reveal the need to remain committed.

What begins must continue, and what continues faithfully will finish well.

A life of faithfulness produces lasting impact and a legacy that honors God.

CLOSING CHARGE

Remain faithful.

Remain when it is difficult.

Remain when it is unnoticed.

Remain when it is inconvenient.

Guard your walk with God. Stay grounded in truth. Stay connected to the Body.

What you do consistently will determine how you finish.

Do not drift. Do not compromise. Do not quit.

Finish what God has called you to do.

REFLECTIVE QUESTIONS

1. What does faithfulness look like in my life right now?

2. How do I respond when I feel weary or discouraged?

3. Am I guarding my relationship with God daily?

4. What areas of my life require greater consistency?

5. Am I committed to finishing well, no matter the cost?

PRAYER

Lord, help me to remain faithful in every season of my life.

Strengthen me when I am weary, guide me when I am uncertain, and keep me grounded in Your truth.

Guard my heart from pride, compromise, and discouragement.

Teach me to walk with You daily so that I may finish well and fulfill what You have called me to do.

In Jesus' Name, Amen.

EPILOGUE

THE CALL STILL STANDS

The call of God has not changed.

It has not weakened.

It has not lowered its standard.

It still calls for faithfulness.

God is not looking for perfection—

He is looking for **consistency.**

Not what you do occasionally,

but what you do continually.

Faithfulness is proven over time.

There will be difficult days.

There will be moments of weariness.

But the call remains:

Remain consistent.

Remain in prayer.

Remain in obedience.

Remain in truth.

Your life is being shaped daily—

by what you do repeatedly.

In the end, the question will not be:

How much did you do?

But:

Were you faithful?

Many start strong.

Few remain consistent.

So, walk forward.

Stay disciplined.

Stay obedient.

Stay faithful.

Be faithful.

Be consistent.

Because in the end,

consistency proves your faithfulness.

ABOUT THE AUTHOR

Elder Joel Latimore Jr. has been called into the ministry for over forty years. His teaching and writing reflect a life shaped by Scripture, testing, correction, and the faithful hand of God over time.

Through both experience and conviction, he emphasizes that the call of God is not proven in moments, but in faithfulness and consistency. His message challenges believers to move beyond desire and into disciplined obedience, spiritual maturity, and a life governed by truth.

Elder Joel Latimore Jr. writes to equip ministers and believers to walk in alignment with God, remain steadfast through every season, and carry their calling with seriousness and integrity.

www.ingramcontent.com/pod-product-compliance
Lightning Source LLC
Chambersburg PA
CBHW070136100426
42743CB00013B/2726